YOUR KNOWLEDGE HAS VALUE

- We will publish your bachelor's and master's thesis, essays and papers

- Your own eBook and book - sold worldwide in all relevant shops

- Earn money with each sale

Upload your text at www.GRIN.com and publish for free

Sardar Imran Hussain Bali

A Book Review of "A Mirror For Our Times" by Paul Weller

GRIN Verlag

Bibliografische Information der Deutschen Nationalbibliothek:

Die Deutsche Bibliothek verzeichnet diese Publikation in der Deutschen National-
bibliografie; detaillierte bibliografische Daten sind im Internet über http://dnb.d-
nb.de/ abrufbar.

Dieses Werk sowie alle darin enthaltenen einzelnen Beiträge und Abbildungen
sind urheberrechtlich geschützt. Jede Verwertung, die nicht ausdrücklich vom
Urheberrechtsschutz zugelassen ist, bedarf der vorherigen Zustimmung des Verla-
ges. Das gilt insbesondere für Vervielfältigungen, Bearbeitungen, Übersetzungen,
Mikroverfilmungen, Auswertungen durch Datenbanken und für die Einspeicherung
und Verarbeitung in elektronische Systeme. Alle Rechte, auch die des auszugsweisen
Nachdrucks, der fotomechanischen Wiedergabe (einschließlich Mikrokopie) sowie
der Auswertung durch Datenbanken oder ähnliche Einrichtungen, vorbehalten.

Imprint:

Copyright © 2013 GRIN Verlag GmbH
Druck und Bindung: Books on Demand GmbH, Norderstedt Germany
ISBN: 978-3-656-48554-4

This book at GRIN:

http://www.grin.com/en/e-book/231799/a-book-review-of-a-mirror-for-our-times-
by-paul-weller

GRIN - Your knowledge has value

Der GRIN Verlag publiziert seit 1998 wissenschaftliche Arbeiten von Studenten, Hochschullehrern und anderen Akademikern als eBook und gedrucktes Buch. Die Verlagswebsite www.grin.com ist die ideale Plattform zur Veröffentlichung von Hausarbeiten, Abschlussarbeiten, wissenschaftlichen Aufsätzen, Dissertationen und Fachbüchern.

Visit us on the internet:

http://www.grin.com/

http://www.facebook.com/grincom

http://www.twitter.com/grin_com

Book Review by:

Sardar Imran Hussain Bali
Electrical and Computer Engineering
Jacobs University Bremen
Class of 2015

Course:

610102- Religious Violence in the Contemporary World

Book:

A Mirror For Our Times
'The Rushdie Affair' and the Future of Multiculturalism

Author:

Paul Weller

Publisher:

New York, London: Continuum International Publishing Group Ltd.

Year:

2009

Pages:

277

Paul Weller's book, *"A mirror for our times- The Rushdie Affair and the Future of Multiculturalism"*, was written on the 20th anniversary of the author, Salman Rushdie's controversially infamous book *'The Satanic Verses'*. Weller's book solely aspires to investigate the repercussion of the 'Rushdie Affair', linking it to the modern era and thus helping in managing such contentious scenarios in regard to diverse, multicultural communities and minorities. The author himself points out, [1] "Author's evaluation of the principle issues at stake, the exploration of which is what the book as a whole is about". Weller finds himself attached to this controversial affair since 1988 (*'The Satanic Verse'* Publishing year*)* when he was employed at the Inter Faith Network for the United Kingdom. Later in 1990, he took up a post at the University of Derby along with a part time doctorial research at the University of Leeds on the 'The Rushdie Affair' and it's consequences. Weller has in fact previously published some books, short works and papers on religious controversies including 'The Rushdie Affair'. *'A mirror for our times'*, is a perfect piece of writing that may attract a variety of individuals including scholarly critics, students and the general public living in the 21st century and facing the social dilemmas such as equality, freedom of religion, speech and expression.

Publication of *'The Satanic Verses'* was foreseen to enrage Muslims globally. Those who warned were well aware of how certain Muslims in particular do not tolerate any insult on their Prophet. They were aware of how these Muslims were willing to go to any extent to deliver justice to the offender as per how they felt without the reference of law. This being the case resulted in the banning of the book, the book burning in Bradford, England and the declaration of Ayatollah Khomeini's fatwa. The predicted reaction of the Muslims was deemed extreme by the western world. This particular event led to intense repercussions and gave rise to questions on the probable Muslim future reactions on such issues such as the 2006 Danish cartoon Affair. Further negative characterization of Muslims was imposed after the Muslim involvement in the 9/11 and the 7/7 events were confirmed. Such condemned events have been characterized as religion driven. This religion extremism, existing even outside Islam, is the reason why liberal, secular states in the west are sought. With the division of such diverse, multicultural communities and the presence of religious dichotomies with varying beliefs and practices, management has always been an issue of debate. Little has been done to improve the situation of co-existence of

---

[1] *'A mirror for our times' Introduction [p.2]*

such communities. Weller's book, as the title suggests, *"A mirror for our times- The Rushdie Affair and the Future of Multiculturalism"*, reflects upon the policy building and the recognition of such diverse societies and their management in terms of equality, judgment and accountability.

The book commences with the author's acknowledgements describing the events that led to the successful publication of the book. Further, the book provides a timeline of the key events mentioned in the book and relating to *'The Rushdie Affair'*. These events provide the reader with a vivid image of the main and in turn consequential events at stake, helping the reader keep track of the chronology. The book additionally proceeds towards the introduction, giving a concise background of the author and his relation to the controversy. Weller even provides a very brief summary of 'The Rushdie Affair' and it's immediate results to set the stage. In it's introduction the book provides important contemporary sources; mainly newspaper articles, journals and book chapters. *"A mirror for our times"* is divided into four primary chapters, each including sections that relate to their primary chapter. Finally, the book ends with a bibliography and a very constructive and effective Index branched into topics, places, individuals and organizations all of which prove to be extremely efficient and useful for the reader.

Rushdie's *'The Satanic Verses'*, the succinct explanation of its profanity, the spark, which ignited the fire, and the immediate probable dilemma that arose are all touched in the first chapter, *"The Contours of the Controversy"*. Weller in the chapter proceeds by building up a background and advances by giving a detailed outline of the developed 'Affair'. Weller while trying to summarize the book, refers to its content as of having, [2]*"phantasmagoric flavor"*. Throughout neutral, the author finds Rushdie's book eclectic and somewhat 'dream-like'. The chapter goes on giving detailed, spell-by-spell insights of the resulting events and the individuals involved. Events such as, the book burning in Bradford, Ayatollah Khomeini's fatwa, the response of the wider world and the violence that prevailed as a result have all been shed light on thoroughly in the chapter. Terminologies, such as a 'Fatwa', which may not be clear to the general reader, are briefly explained. A very critical and significant analysis in the chapter is done on the Muslim reaction on the fatwa and how it gave rise to dialogue amongst the Muslims as the section

---

[2] *'A mirror for our times', The Contours of the Controversy [p.15]*

'Incitement' quotes Mr. Mahmud Lund, [3] *"The clear distinction here is that Rushdie is legally sentenced to death within the guidelines of Islam but he lives in a land where he cannot be legally punished in this way"*. After the production of the chapter outlining the initial details and events, Weller in his following chapter, *"Actions and Reactions in the Controversy"*, yet again provides timely responses to the scenario. Mainly scrutinizing the term 'multiculturalism' and debating on how such crucial issues can hamper the community as a whole. The chapter further provides various reactions of religious groups such as the Christian, Hindu, Sikh and the Buddhist. Weller tries to point how such events develop interfaith differences and how the predicament should be dealt.

The author's main argument throughout has been that the consequent trends of the events that developed after the 'Affair' can be better comprehended by reverting to the original catalyst or the 'magnifying glass', as the books third chapter, *"Through the Looking Glass"*, quotes [4]Bennett, *"The insistent question I find myself asking is this-is it any longer about the book at all or has the book become a catalyst for other, perhaps even more crucial issues?"* This chapter mainly focuses on the law, religion, reforms and the party politics relating to blasphemy and minority rights on such occasions. Weller in the chapter even refutes the multiculturalism failure claims. The chapter quotes [5]Frey Weldon's declaration, "Our attempt at multiculturalism has failed. The Rushdie affair demonstrates it". Weller on the other hand believes that such critiques assume the society to be identical. The chapter further explains how British Muslims lost their trust in the labor party after its support for the publication of the profane book and how new Muslim politicians started to emerge from Independent seats. The final chapter, "Echoes, Reverberations and 'Social Policy Shock'" caters to resolve the present problems associated with multiculturalism. The chapter does so by overlooking the existence of the term as a reason for the establishment of notions such as 'Islamophobia' after the catastrophic 7/7 and 9/11 events. It does however explain these and other consequential events such as the Theo Van Gogh's murder and the cartoon controversy in separate accounts. Weller tries to develop a point that certain extreme groups amongst the society are the reason for the violence, pardoning the majority who are blamed as a result. The chapter tries to conclude with the author presenting key solutions and role of institutions on the opposition of emerging resistance during such events.

---

[3] *'A mirror for our times', The Contours of the Controversy [p.44]*
[4] *'A mirror for our times', Through the Looking Glass [p.102]*
[5] *'A mirror for our times', Through the Looking Glass [p.103]*

Finally the chapter provides points and principles in the hope to deliver recognition to all the parties. Amongst these points Weller stresses on how [6]Muslims and others should reflect on how Muslims and the 'secular' might engage in future. Even though a valid point is developed the author left it vague and not convincing the reader on its implementation.

This book is no doubt a comprehensive account of the actual 'Rushdie Affair' and not the blasphemous book itself. It thoroughly explains the events that followed after or as a result of the 'Affair'. Though the book talks very less about *"The Satanic verses"*, it achieves its soul purpose of delivering a definite description of the scenario and its impact on the 21st century East and West, with the Muslims in context. It is a magnificent piece of well-versed writing, which provides debatable policies that can and should be implemented in our times, in the hope for a peaceful multicultural existence.

Total Words: 1408

---

[6] *'A mirror for our times'*, Echoes, Reverberations and 'Social Policy Shock' *[p.203] Point number 9.*